# THE CLUE
# IS IN
# THE POO

## and other stuff too

Andy Seed

illustrated by Claire Almon

Quarto is the authority on a wide range of topics.
Quarto educates, entertains and enriches the lives of our readers—enthusiasts and lovers of hands-on living.
www.quartoknows.com

Art Director: Susi Martin
Designer: Clare Barber
Editorial Director: Laura Knowles
Editor: Carly Madden
Publisher: Maxime Boucknooghe

Text © Andy Seed 2018
Illustrations and design © Quarto Publishing plc 2018

This edition first published in 2018 by QED Publishing,
an imprint of The Quarto Group.
The Old Brewery, 6 Blundell Street,
London N7 9BH, United Kingdom.
T (0)20 7700 6700 F (0)20 7700 8066
www.QuartoKnows.com

A catalogue record for this book is available from the British Library.
ISBN 978-1-78493-573-3
Manufactured in Dongguan, China TL062018

9  8  7  6  5  4  3  2  1

MIX
Paper from
responsible sources
FSC® C104723

# Contents

# Nature detectives

If you've ever found some mysterious animal tracks in the snow or noticed a footprint in a patch of mud and wondered what made it, then this is the book for you. Wild creatures leave a trail of clues wherever they go. This might be the remains of a meal, a hole in the ground, a tuft of fur or perhaps a pile of droppings. With the help of this book you can learn to read these signs, spot other clues and become a skilled nature detective who can track all kinds of wildlife.

Along the way, you will learn a lot about animals, from tiny caterpillars to huge, clomping African mammals. You'll be able to spot signs of birds, insects, reptiles and many other kinds of creatures too and, maybe best of all, you can have fun doing it. So, put on your shoes, grab a camera, head outside and find that poo!

## THE RULES OF TRACKING

**1** Don't disturb any living creature or its home, for example do not touch birds' nests or eggs.

**2** Avoid using bare hands to touch things which might be covered in unwanted bacteria such as poo, pellets, animal remains and feathers.

**3** When collecting items use gloves, tweezers or a polythene bag turned inside out.

**4** Take extra care where there may be dangerous animals about: always go with an experienced, trusted adult.

**5** Only track animals in places where you have permission to go.

4

# A tracker's tools

A sharp pair of eyes is the most important thing you'll need when tracking signs of animals, but it might also help to take along these:

### Small backpack
To keep everything in so that your hands are free. Also useful for keeping your pickled pumpkin sandwiches dry!

### Camera or phone

There are often clues or tracks that you can't identify on the spot. Taking photos gives you the chance to keep a record of something so you can research it later.

### Notebook and pencil
With these two low-tech wonders, you can sketch, take notes, record the size of things and jot down important facts such as where and when you saw something. Notes are also fun to look back on.

### Small polythene bags
The self-seal ones are particularly good for all those things you'll want to collect: owl pellets, nibbled nut shells, rare feathers or a moose skeleton (good luck finding a bag that big).

### Tape measure or ruler

If you discover a very exciting animal footprint you can't take it with you, but you can measure it to help find out which creature left it. You can also take a photo of the clue with the ruler next to it for scale.

### Small magnifying lens
There's no need to haul around a hefty Sherlock Holmes-style magnifying glass. You can get a small but powerful folding lens quite cheaply which will help you to see vital details.

### Small torch
Great for peering into burrows or holes in tree stumps. Also useful if it gets dark!

### Tweezers
Use these to pick up small items that you don't want to touch with bare hands.

### A stick
Vital for poking things! If you come across the body of an animal and want to look for signs of a predator then you need a strong stick. No need to buy one – pick one up in the woods.

### Binoculars
Not essential, but helpful for looking at birds, fleeing animals and, well, anything interesting in the distance.

### Survival stuff
It's probably best to have all of this too:
- Water
- Snack
- Tissues or wet wipes
- Coat, hat or wellies if it's cold, wet or muddy.

**THINGS NOT TO TAKE**
A beach ball
A ladder
A noisy little brother or sister
A piano
A herd of wildebeest

**FOX**
8–11 cm

**WOLVERINE**
14–18 cm

# Poo is good

Poo is good if you are searching for signs of animals. All creatures produce waste and what they leave behind can help us to identify them – poo is a clue! Okay, sometimes it's smelly and covered in flies but many animal droppings don't pong much at all, and it's amazing what you can learn from them.

## What is poo?

Poo is made up of the parts of food that the animal can't digest such as bone, fur, feathers and hard seed cases.

It also contains water, mucus, cells and lots of bacteria.

Poo is waste but to many animals it is also a way of leaving scent and marking their territory.

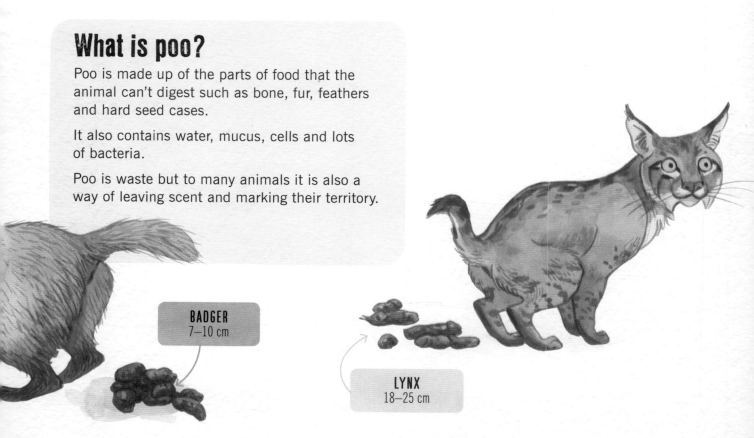

**BADGER**
7–10 cm

**LYNX**
18–25 cm

**WOLF**
12–15 cm

# The bigger the animal the bigger the POO

Big creatures do big poos! When you are out and about, the size of any wild animal droppings you find gives you a clue to the size of the animal. Here is a guide to some big poos to get you started!

**BISON**
20–30 cm

**RHINO**
50–90 cm

**WILD BOAR**
7–8 cm

# BIG poos

If you want to be a top tracker of animals and know what kind of wildlife is around then you need to be able to distinguish doo-doo! Here are some poo pointers plus some amazing facts about huge stools (and I don't mean those high chairs you sit on at breakfast!).

## Really big poos

- Elephants poo about 70 kg a day (that's as heavy as a grown man).
- Giraffe poo falls a long way but it's made up of tiny pellets (so watch where you're standing!).
- Blue whales can leave a plume of poo in the ocean up to 20 m long – be careful where you swim!

- In 2014 a one-metre-long dinosaur poo was sold at an auction, although some scientists argue that this wasn't really a plop at all.
- Scientists have calculated that the largest dinosaur, Argentinosaurus, did about 15 litres of poo at a time.

## Types of turd

**TUBULAR**
Carnivores

**LUMPS**
Herbivores

**PEA-LIKE**
Rabbit family

**PANCAKES**
Cow family

**SHINY BLOCKS/CLUMPS**
Deer

**TWISTED/HAIRY**
Stoat family

Here are the main sorts of mammal poo. But beware, it's easy to confuse poos!

# Little poos

Smaller animals tend to leave little piles of compact, grain-like poos rather than single squashy plops. Telling whose poo is whose is not easy, though. This page will help you to become a mini doo-doo detective!

## Poodunnit?

### Spotty windows

Little dark spots on and around windows in your home are probably tiny fly or spider poos. They are often seen in the corners.

### Pencil lead in your shed?

This is a sign that you probably have house mice visiting. They leave piles of small dark cylinders like rice grains, about 6 mm long and 2 mm thick.

### Pea-pellet poo piles

Rabbits leave scattered piles of centimetre-sized ball-shaped droppings all over grassy areas in the countryside.

## MORE MINI POOS

* Brown rat poos: 12–15 mm
* Wood mouse poos: 5–6 mm
* hare poos: 13–15 mm
* Shrew poos: 2–4 mm
* Vole poos: 6–7 mm

### A loo in your loft?

Heaps of small, dark crumby pellets in a roof space may be the sign of bats.

OWL

HAWK

# Bird doings

Birds don't wee! Instead, their liquid waste and solids are mixed so that their poo often comes out runny. Bird droppings are usually more difficult to identify than mammal poo because so many are small and white.

GULLS

WOODPECKER

CORMORANT

CANADA GEESE

## Your guide to bird plops

Many birds leave a 'fried egg'-type poo including blackbirds, thrushes and pigeons.

PIGEON

PHEASANT

CANADA GOOSE

## Hoot dunnit?

White marks under a tree may be a sign of a roosting owl up above.

## Jet jobbies

Hawks such as buzzards squirt out their poo in a watery stream.

## Deadly droppings

Cormorants have a fish-only diet which gives them nasty acid poo. When they nest in trees these deadly droppings will kill any plants growing underneath.

## Toilet sign

Swallows often leave a pile of white droppings under the nests they make on buildings.

SWALLOWS

PHEASANTS

Oi! I'm going to tweet about this!

HERON

PIGEON

DUCK

GROUSE

GULL

GREEN WOODPECKER

OWL

# Do bears poo in the woods?

Bears that live in the woods poo in the woods. Finding bear poo in the wild is a good way to know that bears are around: POO IS A CLUE!

## Reading doo-doo

Bear droppings can tell us all sorts of things:

- What the bear ate: you might see seeds or bits of hair
- Where the bear is finding food: fish bones suggest water
- Where the bear is living
- How healthy the bear is.

It's not as stinky as it looks!

This BEAR likes scoffing red berries!

## Things bears eat

Here are a few of the favourite things on a bear's menu. Fancy a nibble?

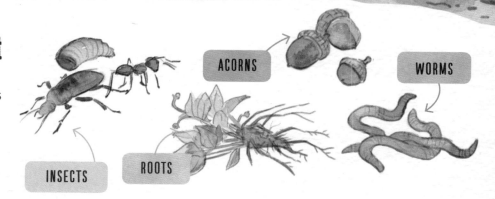

ACORNS

WORMS

INSECTS

ROOTS

## Other signs of bears

**1** Tracks (the footprints are up to 30 cm long)

**2** Holes dug out of the earth, often to find roots

**3** Ant nests which have been destroyed

**4** Claw marks on trees

BROWN BEARS can grow 2.5 metres long and weigh as much as seven adult humans.

FISH

BERRIES

RATS

DEAD MOOSE

# Dinosaur doo-doo

There may no longer be living dinosaurs around dropping massive piles of muck for people to find (despite what Hollywood would like us to believe), but the dinos that lived millions of years ago did leave poos which have now turned to stone and can be dug up. These fossilized faeces are called coprolites.

## Stegosaurus stool or microraptor motion?

It's very hard to identify a dinosaur from its fossil poo, even for experts, but there are certain clues to look out for:

**1** The size of the coprolite: the bigger the dino, the bigger the droppings.

**2** The shape of the coprolite: for example, fossil remains show that prehistoric sharks had twisted rectums and so a spiral poo is almost certainly from one of these extinct giant fish.

**3** Some dinosaurs lived in herds and their poos are found in clusters.

**4** Fossil plops often include evidence of the dino's diet. For example, carnivore coprolites usually contain fossilized bits of bone, teeth and claws whereas herbivore poos are only made up of plant remains.

Do you mind? I was going to the loo!

PACHYCEPHALOSAURUS

## Where to find coprolites

Sadly they aren't easy to find. Good places to look are:

• Areas where there are lots of fossils

• On beaches with cliffs

• In riverbeds

CRETOXYRHINA

## Ancient excrement

Dinosaur coprolites come in all shapes and sizes, but it's often impossible to work out what dino they came from. Here are a few.

14

MICRORAPTOR

ALAMOSAURUS

TRICERATOPS

TYRANNOSAURUS REX

Best poo
I ever did.
Look after it.

## Coprolite facts

- The word *coprolite* means 'dung-stone'.
- Coprolites are literally rock-hard!
- Some of them are 240 million years old.
- Not all coprolites are from dinosaurs – some are poos of other ancient animals and even early people!

## If extinct, does it stink?

Some coprolites might look pongy but, like most rocks, they have no smell at all.

T-REX

# Facts about faeces

You do it, animals do it, everyone does it, but how much do you know about poo? Here are some more fascinating facts about the world of wildlife waste!

## Toilet trivia

- Hyena poo is often white because they eat so many bones.
- A rabbit can produce 500 poo pellets in a day.
- Sloths only poo once a week. They dig a hole in the ground and bury it, too.
- A rhino does enough poo in a year to fill 36 bathtubs.
- Canada geese poo every 20 minutes.
- Hippos sometimes spray their poo around, flapping their tails to make it fly farther.

## Strange doings

- **Parrotfish** often eat hard coral when searching for food. As a result, their poos are full of sand!
- **Some caterpillars** stick poo to their backs as camouflage against hungry birds.

- **Froghopper** nymphs are insects which blow bubbles out of their bottoms. The white froth they make (known as cuckoo spit) helps them hide from predators.

- **Ants** love nothing better than eating sweet, sticky aphid poo.

Wow, a walking poo!

# Oi! Get off my land!

Farmers are supposed to shout this, but did you know that foxes do too? Well, they don't use words but instead say it with poo! Here are the facts:

- Like many animals, foxes mark their territory by leaving poo as a sign to others to keep away.

- A large number of animals also use urine (wee) to claim territory. This is called scent-marking.

- Most mammals have a very good sense of smell, so they can detect the droppings of their rivals while far away.

- Animals can often gain a lot of information by sniffing another animal's poo or wee: what sex and age the animal is, for example.

# You have been warned!

The gross smell of some poo is a chemical warning that it contains harmful bacteria.

# Who dung it?

How good are you at identifying animal poo? Use the knowledge you've gained from this chapter to guess the animal that did the poo in this mucky multiple-choice quiz. Check your score at the end!

## Whose POO?

### 1

a. cow     c. sheep
b. horse     d. pig

### 2

a. osprey     c. grouse
b. swan     d. wren

### 3

a. water vole     c. cat
b. weasel     d. fox

### 4

a. leopard     c. snake
b. crocodile     d. elephant

### 5

a. slug     c. fly
b. frog     d. worm

### 6

a. beaver     c. otter
b. elk     d. mink

## DUNG score

*Get it while it's hot!*

| YOUR SCORE | RATING |
| --- | --- |
| 6 | Poo-tastic! You truly are the number one when it comes to number twos! |
| 4 – 5 | Just the jobbie! That's top-notch idumpification. |
| 2 – 3 | Well dung! At least you're not, er, bottom of the pile. |
| 0 – 1 | Oh poo… Perhaps you'd better read this chapter again. And take that blindfold off. |

Answers on page 64

# Dangerous things to track: LIONS

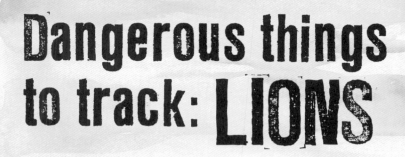

Most lions live in Africa, with some native to parts of Asia too. They usually live in groups, hunting together most often at night. Expert rangers track lions and know what to look for – and how to avoid becoming lion lunch!

## Signs of lions

- A gathering of vultures or hyenas is often a sign that lions have been feeding
- A carcass of a partly eaten antelope, zebra or giraffe
- Lion poo: this will look like very large cat poo
- Lion tracks: lions have large padded footprints 90–140 mm long

## Rules for tracking lions

- No running
- Walk quietly – lions sleep a lot and you don't want to wake them
- Avoid dense bushes and tall, thick grass – you could stumble right onto a lion
- Keep extra distance from lions with cubs

## If you get too close...

- Stand still
- Back slowly away
- Throw rocks or sticks if the lion charges

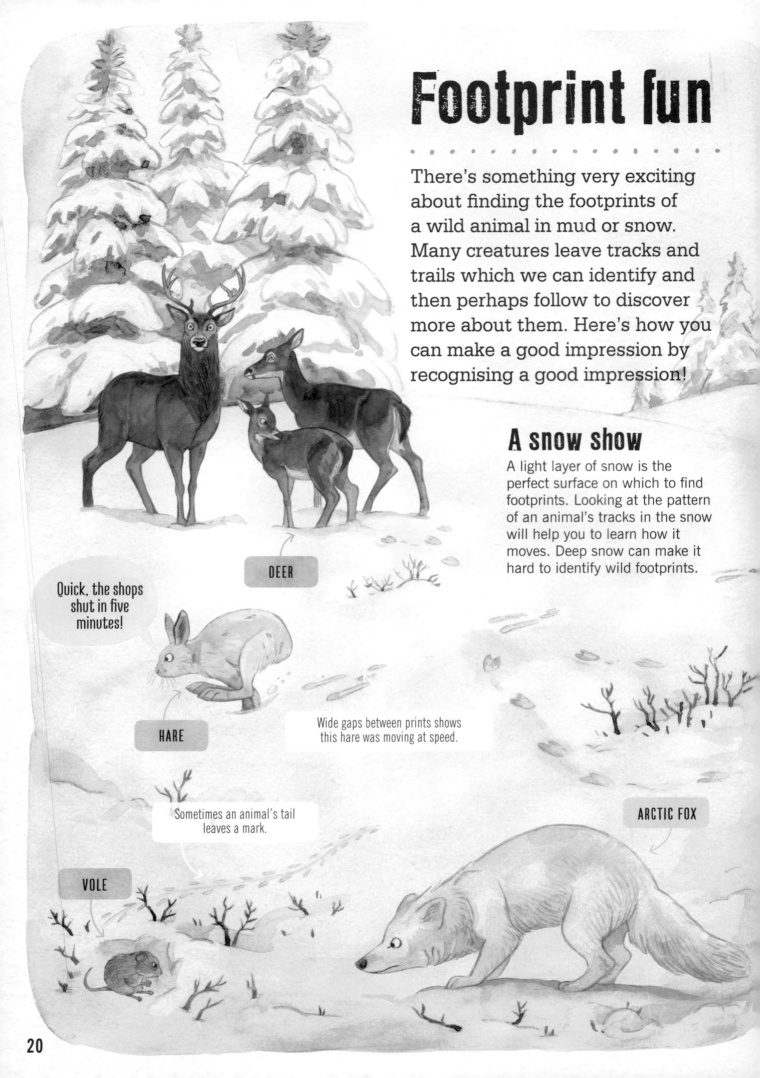

# Footprint fun

There's something very exciting about finding the footprints of a wild animal in mud or snow. Many creatures leave tracks and trails which we can identify and then perhaps follow to discover more about them. Here's how you can make a good impression by recognising a good impression!

## A snow show

A light layer of snow is the perfect surface on which to find footprints. Looking at the pattern of an animal's tracks in the snow will help you to learn how it moves. Deep snow can make it hard to identify wild footprints.

DEER

Quick, the shops shut in five minutes!

HARE

Wide gaps between prints shows this hare was moving at speed.

ARCTIC FOX

Sometimes an animal's tail leaves a mark.

VOLE

# RECORDING FOOTPRINTS

If you find a really great set of footprints and want to identify the animal, you can sketch them, measure them and photograph them close-up.

A good footprint in mud will reveal pads, toes and maybe even claws.

## Trails

Where animals make repeated journeys in one place they often leave a trail or track like a narrow path. This may lead to a burrow or feeding area.

Muddy shores are good for spotting bird trails but beware of deep sticky mud!

## Mud is good

Animals walking across thin layers of mud often leave very clear footprints. Look around the edges of ponds and puddles, or shallow ditches in woods. Wet sand is also a good place to search for tracks.

21

# Know your feet

Animals come in all shapes and sizes, and so do their feet. A little knowledge about the different types of feet found across the natural world can enable the wildlife enthusiast to do some dazzling detective work. This handy (or rather footy) guide is just what you need...

## Well padded

Many mammals, such as badgers, weasels, rabbits and squirrels, have soft but strong pads on the underside of their feet. The shapes of these can sometimes be seen in their footprints.

## Flat-footed animals

**EXAMPLES** Badger, shrew, otter, hedgehog, stoat, human

**INFO** These animals put the whole of their feet down when they walk. Five toes are visible in the footprint.

BADGER

HYENA

## Tiptoe walkers

**EXAMPLES** Cat, dog, wolf, hyena, lynx

**INFO** These animals move on their toes. They are usually faster than flat-footed creatures.

## Cloven-hooved

**EXAMPLES** Deer, boar, elk, sheep, goat, cow

**INFO** These animals walk on two large, flat toes called hooves.

PANDA

DEER

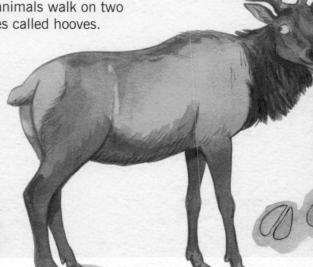

SEA EAGLE

# Single hoof

**EXAMPLES** Horse, donkey

**INFO** These animals walk on just one toe! They have long legs but no other toes.

CROW

DONKEY

# Perching birds

**EXAMPLES** Pigeon, crow, sparrow, pheasant, osprey

**INFO** These birds have feet with three toes pointing forward and one backwards. The toes have curved claws to help them grip.

# Killer foot

Eagles' feet have huge, sharp claws called talons, powerful enough to kill prey.

# Multi-purpose

Frogs have large, five-toed webbed rear feet. These help them to swim and to jump, as well as grip damp surfaces.

FROG

# Waterbirds

**EXAMPLES** Duck, goose, swan, tern

**INFO** These birds have webbed feet with a thin membrane between the front toes to help them paddle in water.

SWAN

23

# Mammal tracks

Mammals can be very small or enormous (and all the sizes in between), and have padded feet, claws or hooves. This means that they leave behind a huge range of footprints. But fear not; if you want to identify some mammal tracks then these pages will be your guide.

**SHREW**
0.5–1.5 cm

**WATER VOLE**
1–2.5 cm

## Small mammals

Many small mammals hop rather than walk so their prints tend to appear in close pairs. Here are the tracks of a few common critters you might find in towns and countryside.

Mice and other very small mammals are so light that they rarely leave footprints.

**HEDGEHOG**
2.5–3.5 cm

Hedgehog footprints are star-shaped.

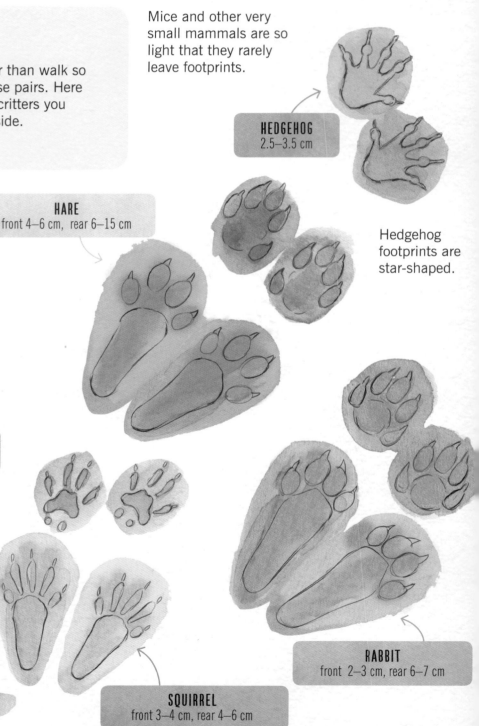

**WOOD MOUSE**
1–2 cm

**HARE**
front 4–6 cm, rear 6–15 cm

**BROWN RAT**
2–4 cm

**RABBIT**
front 2–3 cm, rear 6–7 cm

**SQUIRREL**
front 3–4 cm, rear 4–6 cm

24

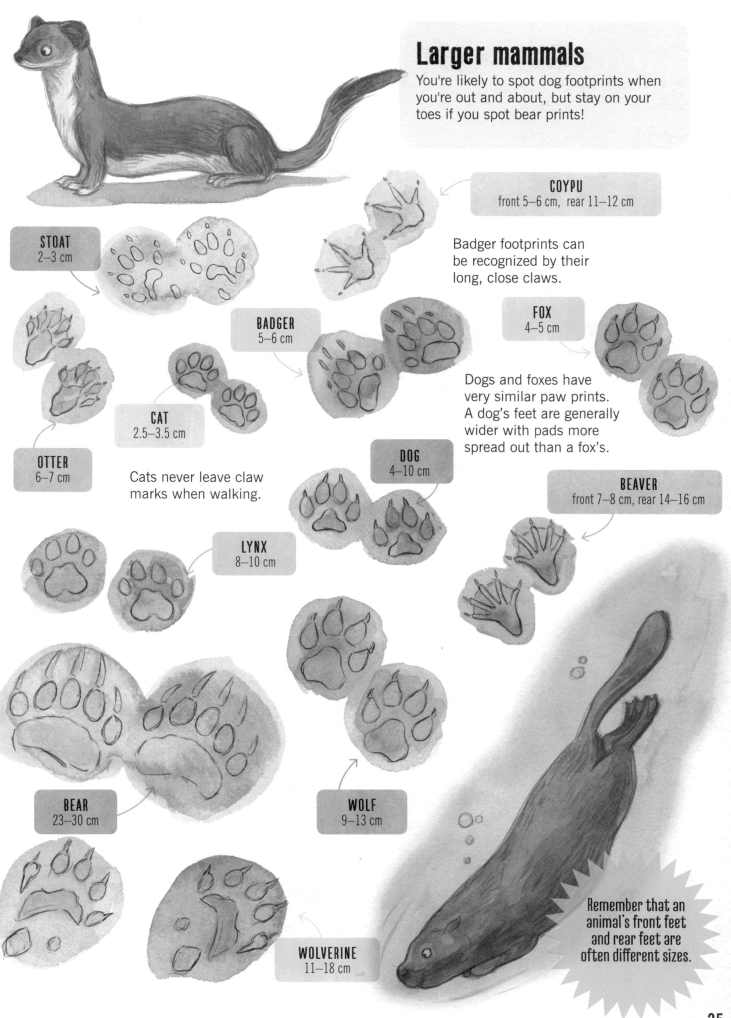

# Larger mammals

You're likely to spot dog footprints when you're out and about, but stay on your toes if you spot bear prints!

**COYPU**
front 5–6 cm, rear 11–12 cm

Badger footprints can be recognized by their long, close claws.

**STOAT**
2–3 cm

**FOX**
4–5 cm

**BADGER**
5–6 cm

Dogs and foxes have very similar paw prints. A dog's feet are generally wider with pads more spread out than a fox's.

**CAT**
2.5–3.5 cm

**DOG**
4–10 cm

**OTTER**
6–7 cm

**BEAVER**
front 7–8 cm, rear 14–16 cm

Cats never leave claw marks when walking.

**LYNX**
8–10 cm

**BEAR**
23–30 cm

**WOLF**
9–13 cm

**WOLVERINE**
11–18 cm

Remember that an animal's front feet and rear feet are often different sizes.

# Mammals with hooves

Look out for these prints around farms and woodland.

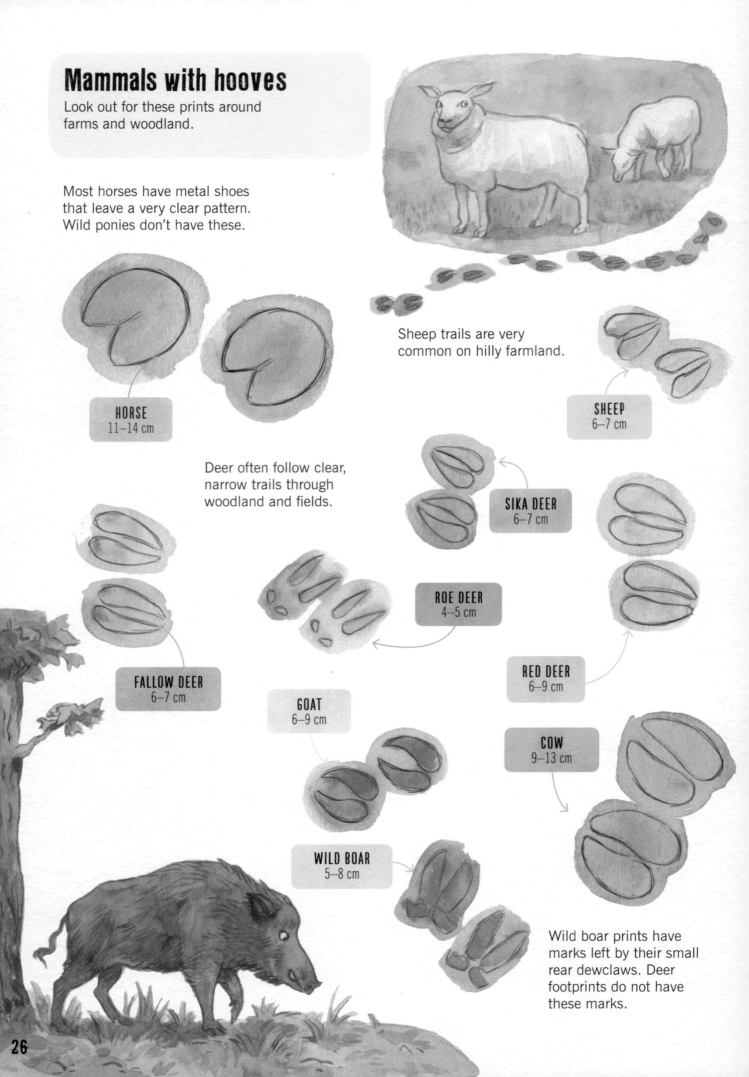

Most horses have metal shoes that leave a very clear pattern. Wild ponies don't have these.

**HORSE**
11–14 cm

Sheep trails are very common on hilly farmland.

**SHEEP**
6–7 cm

Deer often follow clear, narrow trails through woodland and fields.

**SIKA DEER**
6–7 cm

**FALLOW DEER**
6–7 cm

**ROE DEER**
4–5 cm

**RED DEER**
6–9 cm

**GOAT**
6–9 cm

**COW**
9–13 cm

**WILD BOAR**
5–8 cm

Wild boar prints have marks left by their small rear dewclaws. Deer footprints do not have these marks.

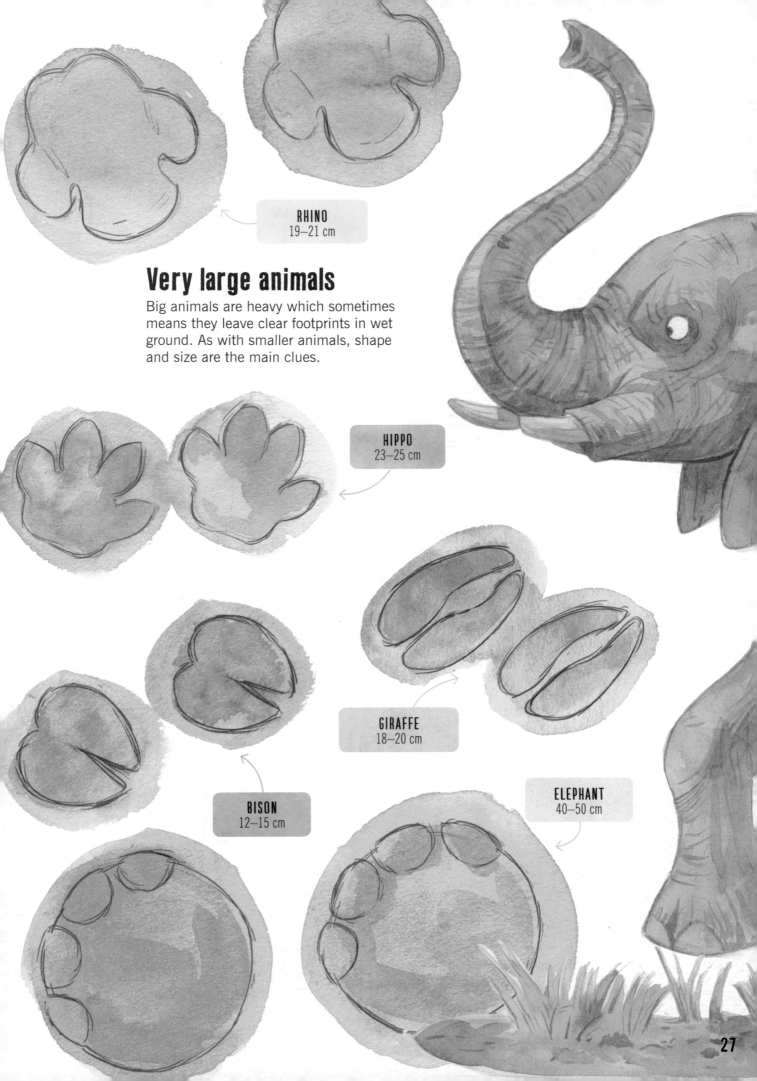

**RHINO**
19—21 cm

## Very large animals

Big animals are heavy which sometimes means they leave clear footprints in wet ground. As with smaller animals, shape and size are the main clues.

**HIPPO**
23—25 cm

**GIRAFFE**
18—20 cm

**BISON**
12—15 cm

**ELEPHANT**
40—50 cm

# Bird tracks and other trails

Birds have four toes, usually with three pointing forwards and one backwards. Waterbirds also have webbed feet, which often makes their footprints easier to recognise. On the other hand, most small birds are so light that they rarely leave trails at all!

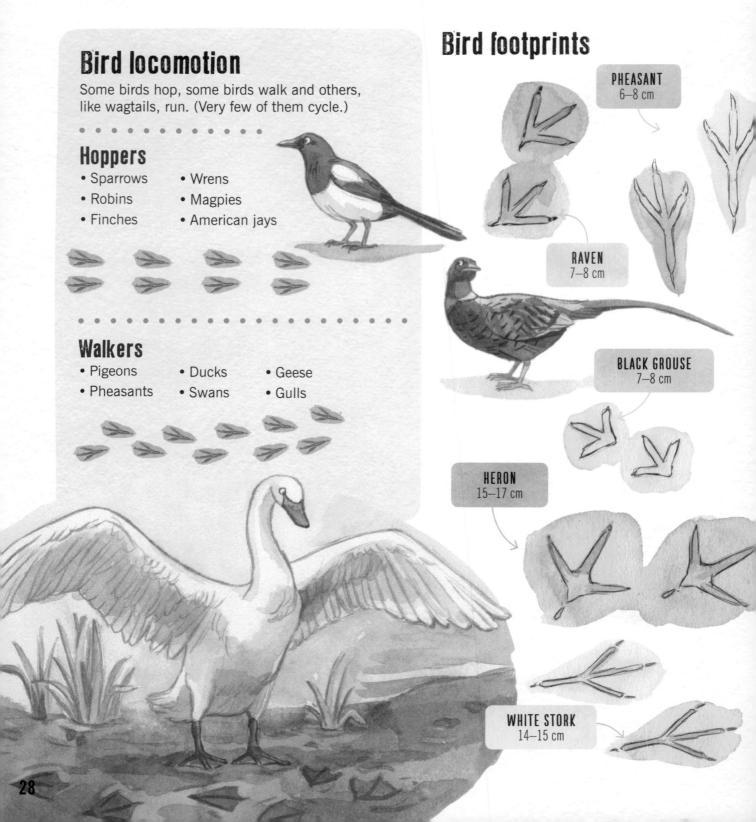

## Bird locomotion

Some birds hop, some birds walk and others, like wagtails, run. (Very few of them cycle.)

### Hoppers
- Sparrows
- Robins
- Finches
- Wrens
- Magpies
- American jays

### Walkers
- Pigeons
- Pheasants
- Ducks
- Swans
- Geese
- Gulls

## Bird footprints

PHEASANT
6–8 cm

RAVEN
7–8 cm

BLACK GROUSE
7–8 cm

HERON
15–17 cm

WHITE STORK
14–15 cm

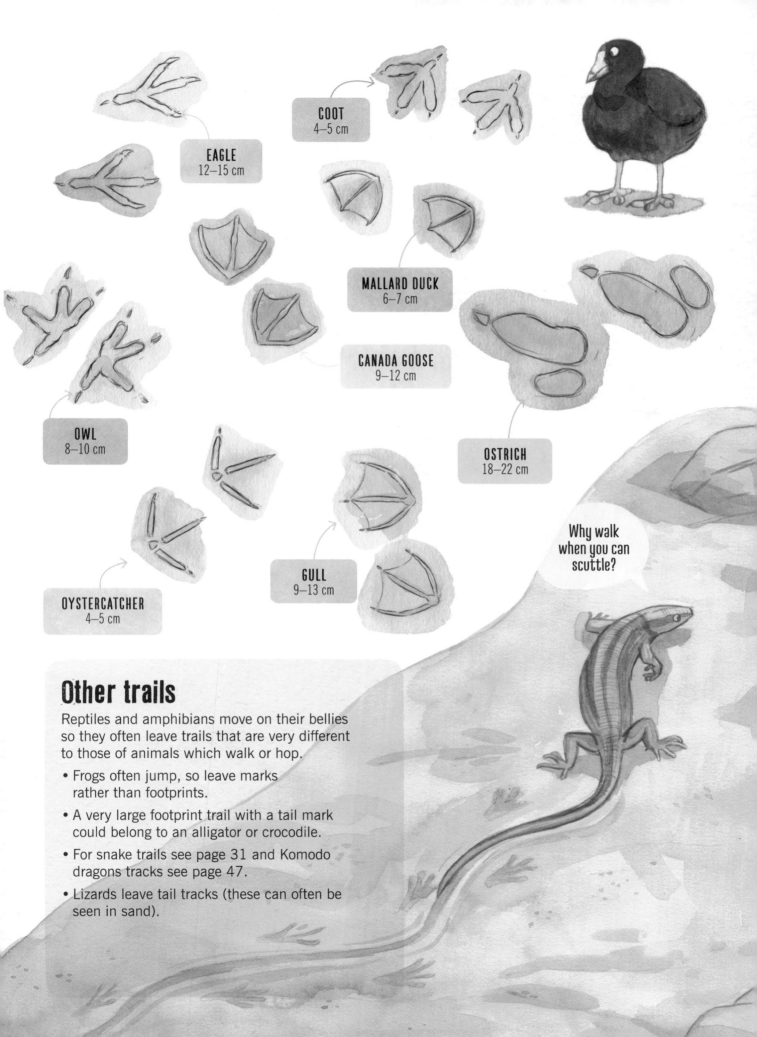

**COOT**
4–5 cm

**EAGLE**
12–15 cm

**MALLARD DUCK**
6–7 cm

**CANADA GOOSE**
9–12 cm

**OSTRICH**
18–22 cm

**OWL**
8–10 cm

**GULL**
9–13 cm

**OYSTERCATCHER**
4–5 cm

Why walk when you can scuttle?

# Other trails

Reptiles and amphibians move on their bellies so they often leave trails that are very different to those of animals which walk or hop.

- Frogs often jump, so leave marks rather than footprints.

- A very large footprint trail with a tail mark could belong to an alligator or crocodile.

- For snake trails see page 31 and Komodo dragons tracks see page 47.

- Lizards leave tail tracks (these can often be seen in sand).

# Whose footprints are these?

Are you a good animal trail detective? Can you tell a tiger track from a pelican print? Find out by trying this simple quiz!

## Whose FOOTPRINT?

**1**

a. cow     c. bat
b. weasel     d. seal

**2**

a. mink     c. fallow deer
b. kangaroo     d. pig

**3**

a. puffin     c. baboon
b. lark     d. crow

**4**

a. leopard     c. turtle
b. schoolgirl     d. hamster

**5**

a. vulture     c. centipede
b. gull     d. frog

**6**

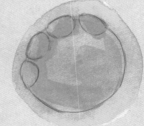

a. mouse     c. camel
b. turkey     d. elephant

## CHECKER chart

*I can never find shoes to fit!*

| YOUR SCORE | RATING |
|---|---|
| 6 | Prince of prints! You're the top tracker in town. |
| 4-5 | Round of 'apaws'! That's great footwork. |
| 2-3 | You're on track and mid-pack, well done. |
| 0-1 | Trailing in at the end... unlucky – if your glasses had been clean you would have got 6. |

Answers on page 64

# Dangerous things to track: SNAKES

Since snakes have an obvious lack of legs they leave trails along the ground rather than tracks. One of the best places to find these shadowy marks is on sand dunes. Watch out for curved lines in a repeated pattern.

## How snakes move

Snakes move in several ways depending upon the species and the ground they are on:

## Snake-tracking facts

- There are over 3,500 types of snake in the world.

- Snakes are cold-blooded, so are not active when the temperature is very high or low.

- Snakes shed their skin and you can sometimes find scraps of old skin (see pages 58–59).

- Snake poos usually look like bird droppings.

WESTERN DIAMONDBACK RATTLESNAKE (N. AMERICA)
Straight line pulses, gripping with scales.

EASTERN BROWN SNAKE (AUSTRALIA)
S-shaped waves which travel from side to side.

INDIAN ROCK PYTHON (ASIA)
Coiled loops, pushing forward to move up slopes.

## Beware!

Snakes should be approached with caution! Different snakes can...

1. Bite
2. Squeeze
3. Poison
4. Spit venom (causing blindness)

# What lives where

Animals live in an amazing variety of places. Some spend their lives in rivers or the sea, and others stay underground or in caves. There is a whole group, the parasites, that live on or in other creatures too (and yes, that includes humans, sorry!). Many animals make their own homes, however, and quite often we can find these and use them as a clue to discover who lives there. Here are some of the places animals live...

> I wish the lodgers wouldn't poo on me.

**CAVE**
Bat, bear, salamander

## Home truths

• Some animals have different winter and summer homes.

• Lots of animals, such as birds, use a home only for breeding.

• Many creatures move home regularly, to avoid being discovered and to maintain food supplies.

• A surprising amount of wildlife shares our own homes. Animals which live in buildings along with people include mice, bats, wasps, ants, spiders, beetles, moths, mites, fleas and flies.

**BEAVER LODGE**
Beaver

# Tree of life

A large oak tree may be home to over 50 species of animals with thousands of minibeasts such as caterpillars, spiders, beetles and aphids living on its trunk, leaves and branches.

Buzz off!

**HOLES IN TREES/LOGS**
Weasel, owl, insect

**NEST**
Bird, wasp, harvest mouse

## Name check

Do you know these names of animal homes?

- Drey – squirrel
- Lodge – beaver
- Warren – rabbit
- Roost – bat
- Form – hare
- Sett – badger
- Holt – otter
- Earth – fox

**BURROW IN THE GROUND**
Rabbit, fox, bee

**MOUND**
Ant, termite

**EARTH**
Worm, slug, grubs

**POND**
frog, newt, water beetle

## Things animal homes do have

* Shelter
* Protection
* A nursery for young
* Food storage

## Things animal homes don't have

* Fitted kitchens
* Power showers
* Doorbells
* Lava lamps
* Wi-fi

# Beasts with burrows

Many animals live underground and their homes can be spotted by the holes they make. If you find an animal burrow look for signs such as the four Fs: faeces, fur, food and footprints. If it's a huge hole, get ready to run!

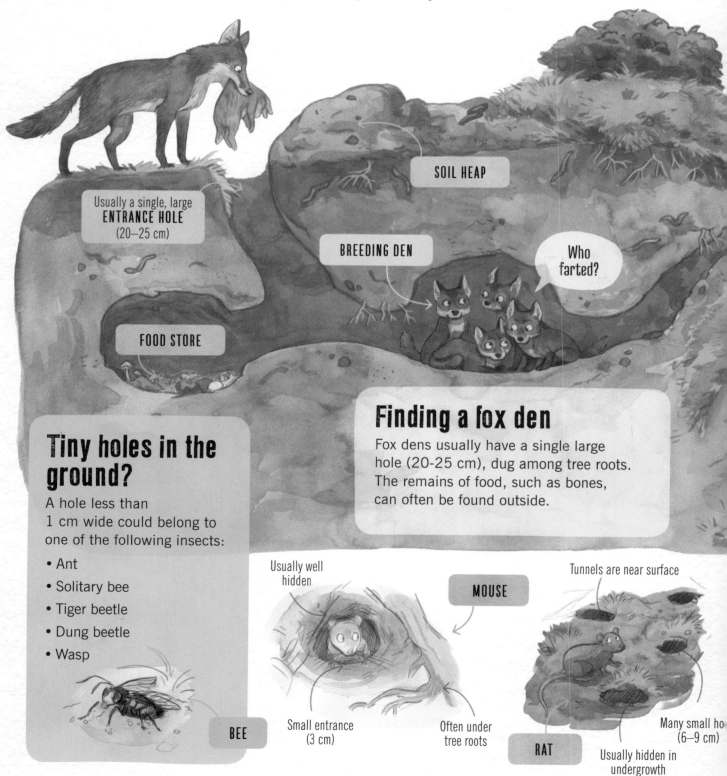

SOIL HEAP

Usually a single, large
**ENTRANCE HOLE**
(20—25 cm)

BREEDING DEN

Who farted?

FOOD STORE

## Tiny holes in the ground?

A hole less than 1 cm wide could belong to one of the following insects:

- Ant
- Solitary bee
- Tiger beetle
- Dung beetle
- Wasp

BEE

## Finding a fox den

Fox dens usually have a single large hole (20-25 cm), dug among tree roots. The remains of food, such as bones, can often be found outside.

Usually well hidden

MOUSE

Tunnels are near surface

Small entrance (3 cm)

Often under tree roots

RAT

Many small ho (6—9 cm)

Usually hidden in undergrowth

34

## Some other burrowers

- Moles
- Shrews
- Meerkats
- Otters
- Gerbils

## These don't live in holes

- Giraffes
- Whales
- T-rex
- Unicorns
- Loch Ness Monster

### BADGER SETT
- Multiple big entrances (20–30 cm)
- Often at the edge of woods
- Large heaps of dug soil outside

### RABBIT WARREN
- Multiple entrances (12–15 cm)
- Often on slopes
- Soil heaps with poo pellets outside

## Birds with burrows

Some birds, such as sand martins and kingfishers, make their nests in holes, often in vertical riverbanks where they can dig out the soft sandy soil with their beaks. Puffins are seabirds which make nests that are short, rabbit-like burrows in soft ground along rocky coasts.

### WATER VOLE

Holes very near to water (5–7 cm)

Often in grassy riverbanks

Some entrances underwater

### PUFFIN

35

# Nest knowledge

Nests are made by birds and other animals as a safe place where babies can be born and grow. They are really a kind of temporary home, hopefully hidden from predators and strong enough to survive harsh weather. Identifying an animal from its nest is quite a challenge!

## Types of nest

### Scrape

A shallow hollow among stones, sand or earth. Examples: Arctic tern, oystercatcher, ringed plover.

### Cup

A bowl-shaped basket made of materials such as twigs, grass and mud. Examples: thrush, robin, blackbird.

### Platform

A big, wide, bulky nest built with large twigs and sticks. Examples: osprey, heron, stork.

### Floating pile

A messy arrangement of plants and grass stems made on water, often among reeds so it can't float away. Examples: coot, moorhen, grebe.

### Sphere

A ball-shaped woven mass of light material such as moss, leaves and hair, with a small entrance hole. Examples: wren, dipper, long-tailed tit.

### Mud pot

Usually found on buildings under an overhanging ledge, these are domes of mud, spit and fine straw. Examples: swallow, house martin.

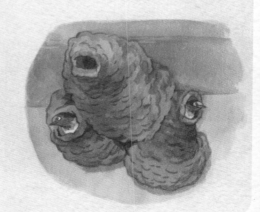

# Features of nests

## Camouflage

Many nests are carefully constructed to blend in with their surroundings. This is to protect the young from predators such as cats.

## Insulation

A lot of animals line the inside of nests with soft materials such as downy feathers, fur or wool to help keep their young warm.

## Location

Birds will make nests in any safe and stable spot, even in strange places like traffic lights!

# Where's the nest?

Lots of birds nest in hedges or bushes, but many don't. Here are some alternative nest spots:

**ROCKS AND CRAGS**
Peregrine falcon, raven

**SEA CLIFFS**
Kittiwake, gannet, fulmar

**CHIMNEY**
Jackdaw, stork

**TOP OF TREE**
Rook, crow, heron

**HOLE IN A TREE**
Woodpecker, crested tit

**RIVERBANK HOLE**
Sand martin, kingfisher

## ANIMALS THAT MAKE NESTS

* Birds
* Mice
* Dormice
* Termites
* Wasps
* Bees
* Squirrels
* Voles
* Wood ants

# Minibeast accommodation

If you discover an animal hole smaller than the thickness of a pencil then it was probably made by an insect or other minibeast. But minibeasts don't just make holes: some species can also create mounds, nests and even giant towers of soil!

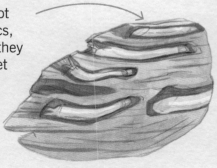

## Bee and wasp holes

Most types of bees and wasps do not live in nests or hives. These solitary insects make small holes, usually in soil, and lay an egg in each one. A larva or grub will grow inside the hole, feeding on food left by the parent.

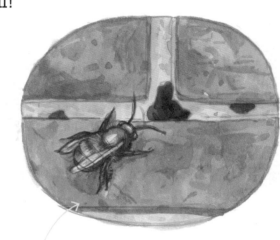

MASON BEE

## Mason Bee

Some types of mason bees lay eggs in holes in brick walls.

WOODWORM

## Holes in wood

These are usually made by the larvae of beetles or moths which eat through wood and bark.

## Miner at work

Mining bees leave neat little piles of soil when they dig holes.

WASP

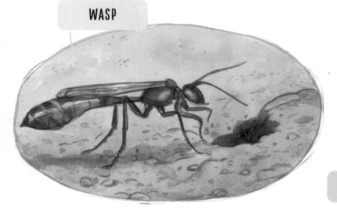

MINER BEE

## Holes at the seashore

**Piddocks** are molluscs with hard shells that 'drill' holes into even harder rocks.

**Shipworms** are not worms but molluscs, with shells which they use to bore into wet wood. In the past they caused many ships to sink!

## Insect skyscraper

Termite mounds in Africa can be over 5 metres tall!

## Minibeasts that make holes

* Bees          * Ants
* Wasps         * Worms
* Hornets       * Termites
* Beetles       * Molluscs

## Pongy holes!

Dung beetles love nothing better than to drag animal poo into a hole to lunch on later.

Why bother with meatballs when you can have pooballs?

TERMITES

DUNG BEETLE

**Lugworms** make holes in wet sand. They leave wiggly worm casts on beaches.

**Gribbles** are tiny crustaceans that munch their way through driftwood (and sometimes piers...).

# Whose home is this?

Do you know your nests from your lodges? Have a go at this home-tastic multiple-choice quiz and see what you score!

## Whose HOME?

**1**

a. chipmunk  c. badger
b. mole      d. moose

**2**

a. harvest mouse  c. fox
b. gull           d. starfish

**3**
a. ants   c. otter
b. bear   d. beaver

**4**

a. woodpecker  c. woodworm
b. eagle       d. bees

**5**

a. earwigs    c. pine marten
b. wood ants  d. cobra

**6**

a. swift   c. toad
b. weasel  d. wasps

> Moose do better!

## CHECKER chart

| YOUR SCORE | RATING |
| --- | --- |
| 6 | Home run! You are a natural naturalist! Top marks. |
| 4 – 5 | Amazing animal architecture awareness! Good for you. |
| 2 – 3 | A 'hole-hearted' effort! Keep reading and learning. |
| 0 – 1 | Hope you do better nest time! |

Answers on page 64

# Dangerous things to track: POLAR BEARS

Polar bears are the largest land carnivores on the planet, with a big male weighing about the same as seven adult humans. They are fast, good swimmers, hugely strong and have big claws so you should probably only track one if you REALLY have to....

## Where are POLAR BEARS found?

Polar bears only live in Arctic areas:

* Canada
* Alaska
* Greenland
* Russia
* Norway

## What makes a POLAR BEAR?

**WHITE FUR** for camouflage

**EXCELLENT SENSE OF SMELL** to locate prey

**STRONG JAWS** for killing seals

**POWERFUL LIMBS** for attack

**SHARP CLAWS** for gripping ice and prey

**THICK LAYER OF FAT** for warmth

**BROAD FEET** for swimming and walking on ice

RUSSIA

NORTH AMERICA

POLAR BEAR RANGE

## Signs to look out for

As well as footprints and droppings, you may find remains of the things they eat:

* Seals (their main diet)
* Fish
* Small whales
* Young walruses
* Birds' eggs
* Crabs

(They also occasionally eat reindeer, birds, plants and people.)

# Signs of munching

Have you ever walked through a forest and found the ragged, well-chewed remains of a pine cone? Well, that's probably the leftovers from a squirrel's lunch. Or it could be a mouse… or a woodpecker. This section will help you to spot all kinds of feeding signs of different plant-eating animals. Read on…

## Barky breakfast

Beavers eat bark and the soft wood found under it. They can fell whole trees with their powerful teeth.

I also do free hedge-trimming.

**LOW BRANCHES BROWSED**
possibly by deer

**TREES CUT INTO**
by beavers

Hmm, tastes a bit woody.

**BARK STRIPPED FROM TREES**
possibly by water voles

**TWIGS BITTEN**
possibly by hares

# Snack time

Nuts, seeds, vegetables and fungi are eaten by a huge range of animals. Many nibble a small part leaving holes or teeth marks.

**CONES MUNCHED**
possibly by mice

**VEGETABLES NIBBLED**
possibly by rats

**FUNGI CHEWED**
possibly by slugs

At last, a restaurant with a view!

# Leafy lunch menu

Most wild animals eat plants and a huge number of them like nothing better than to feast on the leaves of trees, bushes and smaller plants. Looking carefully at the signs of damage can help you to identify just what is lunching on your lupins!

## Neat nibbling

Leafcutter bees remove neat half-circles from leaves to build their nests.

**LEAFCUTTER BEES**

## Caught you!

Turning over a nibbled leaf can sometimes reveal the culprits – often gangs of small caterpillars.

**LEAF MINERS**

**CATERPILLAR**

## Mine's a leaf

Leaf miners are tiny insects that actually eat away inside leaves, often leaving weird patterns as they tunnel.

## You've got the gall...

Strange coloured swellings on leaves are often galls. caused by insects eating away inside.

**GALLS**

# Trail of destruction

Slugs and snails adore fresh green leaves and can consume a whole plant in just a few days. They leave behind slime trails as clues.

## Edge eating

Leaves with ragged pieces missing from the edges may be the work of moth or butterfly larvae or insects such as grasshoppers.

## Cabbage crazy

Large holes pecked in cabbages and similar vegetables are often the work of hungry wood pigeons.

CROPS RAIDED
possibly by groundhogs

GRASS CROPPED
e.g. by rabbits

CATERPILLAR

WOOD PIGEON

GRASSHOPPERS

SLUGS AND SNAILS

**HAZELNUTS SPLIT OPEN**
possibly by squirrels

# Fruit and nutty dessert

Many wild animals rely on fruits, nuts and seeds to keep them alive. These foods are rich in important fats, sugars, vitamins and minerals.

## NUTS ABOUT NUTS!

The following animals love eating nuts:

### Mammals
* Squirrels
* Mice
* Dormice
* Voles
* Chipmunks
* Deer
* Bears

### Birds
* Nuthatches
* Woodpeckers
* Tit family
* Jays
* Magpies
* Jackdaws

**BERRIES REMOVED**
possibly by blackbirds

**NUTS WEDGED IN TREES AND PECKED OPEN**
possibly by birds such as nuthatches or woodpeckers

**APPLES PECKED**
possibly by starlings

**APPLES, PLUMS AND OTHER RIPE FRUIT EATEN**
possibly by mice, voles, wasps or birds

**NEAT HOLES GNAWED IN NUTS**
possibly by mice or other small rodents

# Animal lunch

Being a leftovers detective may seem like a queasy job but it's a top way to learn about wildlife. Have a go at solving these little mysteries.

**1**

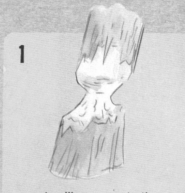

a. caterpillars    c. turtle
b. woodpecker    d. beaver

**2**

a. caterpillars    c. slug
b. spider    d. crocodile

**3**

a. squirrel    c. deer
b. bank vole    d. magpie

**4**

a. deer    c. fox
b. great tit    d. octopus

**5**

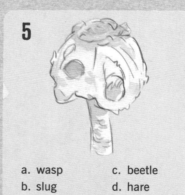

a. wasp    c. beetle
b. slug    d. hare

**6**

a. bat    c. snake
b. stoat    d. squirrel

Anyone for dinner?

CHECKER chart

| YOUR SCORE | RATING |
|---|---|
| 6 | Champ of chomps! An epic piece of dinner detecting. |
| 4–5 | You are a mammal meal master. Excellent! |
| 2–3 | Steady show, so there you go. |
| 0–1 | Oo-er, perhaps you should read the book first? |

Answers on page 64

# Dangerous things to track:
# KOMODO DRAGONS

The biggest lizard in the word is 3 metres long and can swallow a small goat whole. This is the Komodo dragon, found on just four islands in Indonesia. If you want to track one you'd better wear a suit of armour…

## Where are KOMODO DRAGONS found?

INDONESIA

KOMODO RANGE

AUSTRALIA

## Why are Komodo dragons DANGEROUS?

They have vicious serrated teeth and powerful claws.

They can smell prey from 4 km away.

Their bite is both strong and toxic.

They are adapted for stealth attacks.

They can sprint in short bursts.

## Signs to look out for

- Black and white droppings
- Large clawed footprints and tail tracks
- Carcasses of large animals (although Komodo dragons eat bones and guts)
- Large nests with eggs

## What's for dinner?
Komodo dragons will eat any creature they can catch including deer, pigs, birds, monkeys and young Komodos. Attacks on humans are rare but sometimes fatal.

How are the kids?

Delicious.

# Grisly remains

If you find the body of a dead animal, it could have died of natural causes such as old age or disease. Or it could have been killed. You may have a murder mystery to solve! This page will help you to try and discover whodunnit.

CAT

BADGER

MUSKRAT

## A pile of feathers?

A pile of feathers on the ground may be the work of a fox or cat. If the feathers are found on a rock, tree stump or other perch then the unfortunate bird may have been eaten by a hawk or other bird of prey (see p62).

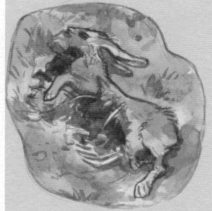

## A pile of skin?

Badgers will often eat smaller animals such as hedgehogs and young rabbits, leaving just the fur and maybe the odd bone, foot or yucky bit of intestine behind.

## Fishy remains?

A partly eaten fish found by a river may have been left by an otter or a mink, muskrat or bear. Ospreys can also be counted as suspects.

# Mussel mess?

Empty black mussel shells on the seashore are usually left by oystercatchers – birds which have several clever techniques for opening these tasty molluscs.

POLECAT

# Frog leftovers?

Lots of animals feed on frogs including buzzards, herons, mink and polecats. Look out for other clues such as footprints, droppings or getaway car tyre tracks (actually, that last one may be wrong…).

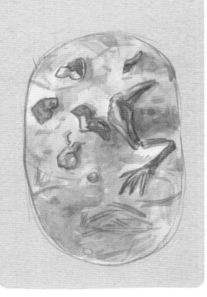

GULL

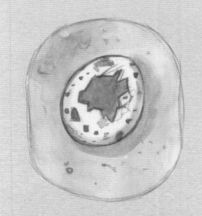

# Empty egg?

An eggshell with a small hole in it is probably evidence of a bird such as a crow or gull. Mammals such as foxes sometimes crush eggs when eating them. Hedgehogs are big fans of an egg for breakfast too!

THRUSH

# Snail shell blitz?

Song thrushes are specialists in smashing snail shells on rocks to provide a meal. Rats, mice and voles also eat snails sometimes.

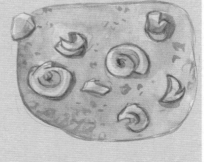

# Skull-duggery

When an animal dies the soft parts of the body will usually either rot away or be eaten, leaving behind the bones. Even when a small animal is swallowed whole by a larger predator the bones are often regurgitated. It is very unusual to find a whole animal skeleton, but finding bones is much easier. This page will help you with the tricky task of identifying them.

## Animal skulls

If you want to identify a skull, note its size and if there is a beak or bill or any teeth attached. The lower jaw of mammals is often separated from the rest of the skull.

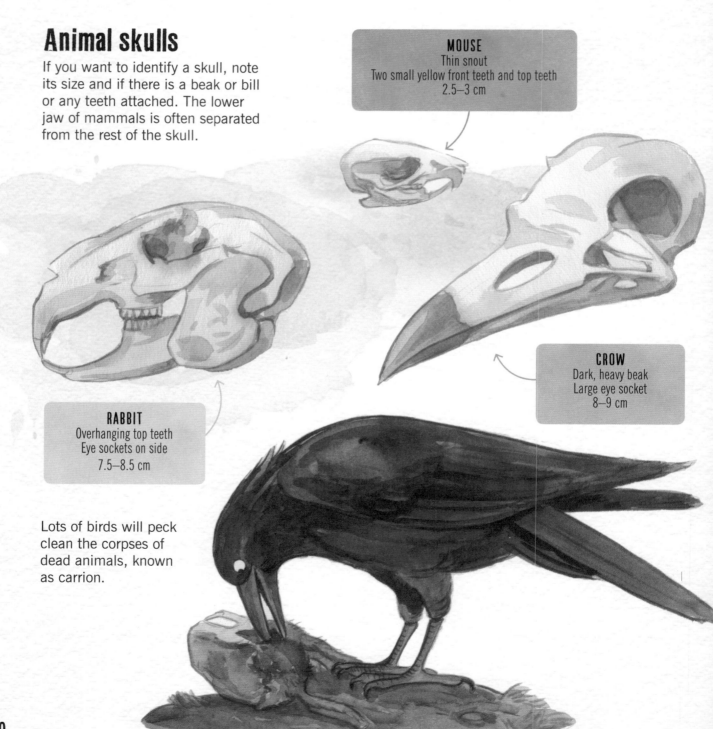

**MOUSE**
Thin snout
Two small yellow front teeth and top teeth
2.5–3 cm

**CROW**
Dark, heavy beak
Large eye socket
8–9 cm

**RABBIT**
Overhanging top teeth
Eye sockets on side
7.5–8.5 cm

Lots of birds will peck clean the corpses of dead animals, known as carrion.

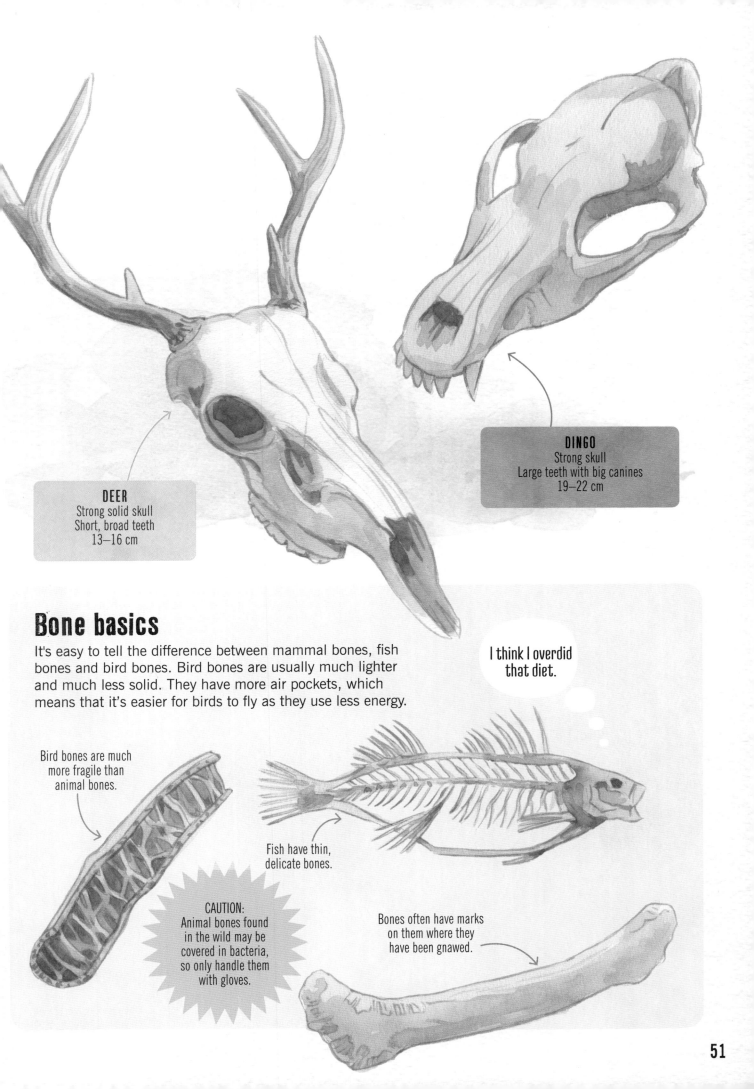

**DINGO**
Strong skull
Large teeth with big canines
19–22 cm

**DEER**
Strong solid skull
Short, broad teeth
13–16 cm

# Bone basics

It's easy to tell the difference between mammal bones, fish bones and bird bones. Bird bones are usually much lighter and much less solid. They have more air pockets, which means that it's easier for birds to fly as they use less energy.

I think I overdid that diet.

Bird bones are much more fragile than animal bones.

Fish have thin, delicate bones.

CAUTION:
Animal bones found in the wild may be covered in bacteria, so only handle them with gloves.

Bones often have marks on them where they have been gnawed.

# Dangerous things to track: WOLVES

Wolves were once much more widespread around the world but they can still be found in places where there are forests and few people or farms. Here is what you need to know...

## Signs of wolves

**1** Droppings like big grey dog poos containing lots of fur.

**2** Footprints like very large dog prints with claws

**3** Gnawed bones and lots of paw marks and blood where a pack has made a kill

**4** Patches of urine left as scent marks

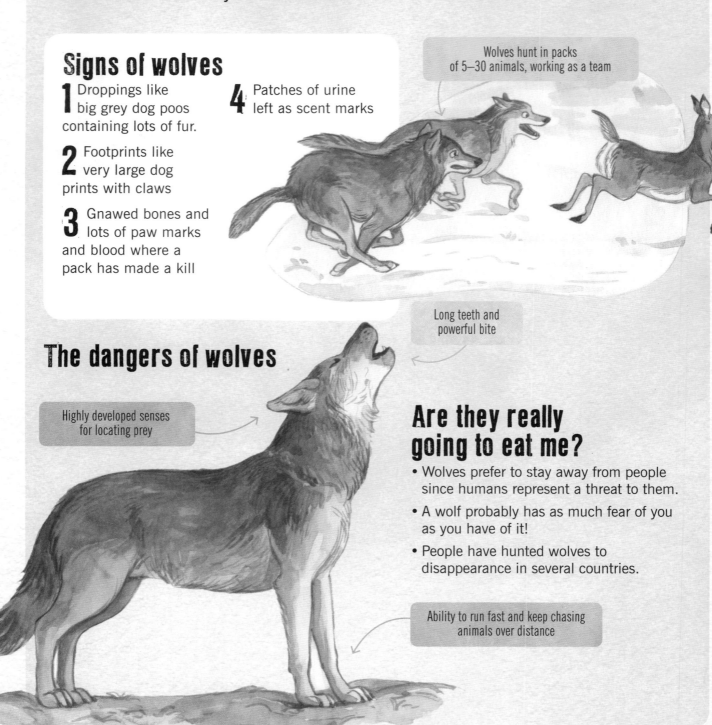

Wolves hunt in packs of 5–30 animals, working as a team

Long teeth and powerful bite

## The dangers of wolves

Highly developed senses for locating prey

## Are they really going to eat me?

- Wolves prefer to stay away from people since humans represent a threat to them.

- A wolf probably has as much fear of you as you have of it!

- People have hunted wolves to disappearance in several countries.

Ability to run fast and keep chasing animals over distance

# Pellet power

Many birds swallow things that they cannot fully digest. These might include mouse bones, chaffinch feathers, rabbit fur, beetle wing cases, mussel shell fragments, cherry stones and grains of sand, among other things. These unwanted items are compressed together in the bird's gizzard (one of its stomachs) then coughed up in the form of a pellet. When we find a pellet we get lots of information about what a bird has eaten.

## Poo or pellet?

Bird pellets do sometimes look like poos. Here's how to tell the difference:

**1** Poos tend to smell more than pellets.

**2** Pellets are nearly always a neat, rounded shape.

**3** Poos are often tapered or twisted.

**4** Pellets often contain bones, but bird poo doesn't.

**5** Poos tend to attract insects.

**6** Pellets are often found under nesting sites or perches.

## If you find a pellet

Put it carefully into a bag. At home, try taking it apart carefully. Do this in a shallow bowl or on a sheet of paper using cocktail sticks, tweezers or something similar. Look for bones and other clues to the bird's diet.

CEREAL HUSKS

HAIR

MUSSEL SHELL FRAGMENTS

CRAB SHELL FRAGMENTS

SMALL FISH BONES

STRING

BEETLE WING CASES

# Your pellet ID guide

If you find a bird pellet then you'll probably want to know what kind of bird it is from. That can be tricky to discover, but a little crafty detection work and the information below will aid you in your quest.

## Bird of prey pellets

- Often contain feather fibres
- Sometimes contain shiny beetle remains
- Some raptors feed on dead sheep, which gives them whiter pellets

**BUZZARD**
(4–5 cm)
Found in Europe and Asia

**TAWNY OWL**
(6–8 cm)
Found in Europe and Asia

**SPARROWHAWK**
(2.5–3.5 cm)
Found in Europe and Asia

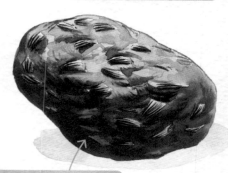

## Owl pellets

- Usually grey or brown
- Contains lots of small bones of voles, birds and other prey
- Matted together with fur and feather remains
- Often found under trees

**STORK**
(4–6 cm)
Found in Europe, North America and northern Asia
(The stork is not a bird of prey but it does eat a wide range of animals including fish.)

# Crow family

- Rooks, magpies, jackdaws and ravens produce rounded pellets
- Often contain plant material such as seeds and grain husks
- Can also contain bones, fur, insect remains and even small stones

**CROW**
(3–4 cm)
Found worldwide

**JACKDAW**
(2–2.5 cm)
Found in Europe, western Asia and North Africa

**ROOK**
(3–4 cm)
Found in Britain and parts of Europe

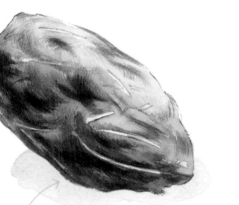

**HERON**
(7–8 cm)
Found worldwide

**BLACK HEADED GULL**
(3–5 cm)
Found in Europe, Asia and parts of Canada

# Gulls

- Often quite round pellets
- Contain a huge variety of material including fish bones, berry pips, beetles and shells
- May even include bits of string and litter

**COMMON GULL**
(5–8 cm)
Found in parts of Europe, Asia and North America

# How do you like your eggs?

Sometimes you may come across a bird's nest full of eggs. If you do, make sure that you leave it undisturbed. Other times, you might find a lonely egg or some bits of eggshell from a nest, odd little insect eggs or jelly-squishy amphibian eggs. All is revealed here!

## Birds' eggs

**CHAFFINCH**
2 cm
Clutch of 4–5 eggs

**ROBIN**
2 cm
Clutch of 4–5 eggs

**COMMON GULL**
5 cm
Clutch of 3 eggs

**TREE SPARROW**
2 cm
Clutch of 5–6 eggs

**CRANE**
9 cm
Clutch of 2 eggs

**MUTE SWAN**
11 cm
Clutch of 5–7 eggs

**BLACKBIRD**
3 cm
Clutch of 3–5 eggs

**MAGPIE**
4 cm
Clutch of 6 eggs

**PHEASANT**
4–6 cm
Clutch of 7–15 eggs

**COMMON NIGHTHAWK**
3 cm
Clutch of 2 eggs

## Do not touch!

It is illegal to remove eggs from nests in many countries, but even just touching them can cause birds to reject them.

**EMU**
13 cm
Clutch of 5–7 eggs

# Cuckoo!

Some types of cuckoo are well known for getting other birds to raise their young. These sneaky 'brood parasites' lay their eggs in another bird's nest (making sure they match in colour) and then let the nest owner incubate the egg and feed the chick. What a cheek!

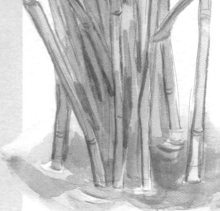

Got any ketchup?

## Other eggs

**BUTTERFLY EGGS**
These tiny eggs can be found on leaves, sometimes single and sometimes in clusters.

**SNAIL AND SLUG EGGS**
These small pale round eggs are usually found in soil.

**SPIDER EGGS**
Many spiders weave silk egg sacs which can be found in corners of buildings.

## Amphibian eggs

These are often found in ponds and lakes in spring.

FROGSPAWN

GREAT CRESTED NEWT EGG

TOAD SPAWN

## Found on the beach

**CUTTLEFISH EGGS**
These look like small bunches of grapes.

**SHARK EGG CASES**
Many small sharks leave behind dark egg cases, sometimes with curly tendrils attached.

**SKATE OR RAY EGG CASES**
These are brown or black square pods with 'horns' and are sometimes called 'mermaids' purses'.

**COMMON WHELK EGG CASES**
These are yellow-white clusters of spongy material.

# Keep your HAIR on

Some animals provide clues that show they are around: they leave behind unwanted parts of their bodies! This is known as moulting and can involve hair, fur, feathers and skin. Some insects and other small creatures even shed their skeleton! As human beings, we also shed our skin and hair, but just a little at a time (it's best not to try and lose it all at once…).

PHEASANT

## Things to look out for

### Feathers
Birds replace damaged feathers, leaving their old ones behind.

### Hare hair
Hares moult every year, leaving behind tufts of their old fur.

### Spider exoskeletons
Spiders shed their skin several times over a lifetime as they grow.

### Snake upgrade
As snakes grow they shed their old skin as it becomes too small. Finding a piece of dry, translucent snake skin means that snakes are about!

Hare today, gone tomorrow.

HARE

WOODLOUSE

BUTTERFLY CHRYSALIS

# Dragonfly drama

Many insects moult as they change from a larva to an adult. The larva or nymph emerges from an egg, grows bigger and then develops a special case (pupa stage) which it then sheds.

NYMPH

ADULT EMERGING

ADULT

MAGPIE

Do you mind? I'm getting changed!

SNAKE

SPIDER

# Feathery finds

Birds replace their feathers with new ones each year and kindly leave the old ones behind for us to collect. These can tell us what kinds of birds are about but sometimes feathers can tell us a lot more, especially if there is a pile of them together and some are damaged...

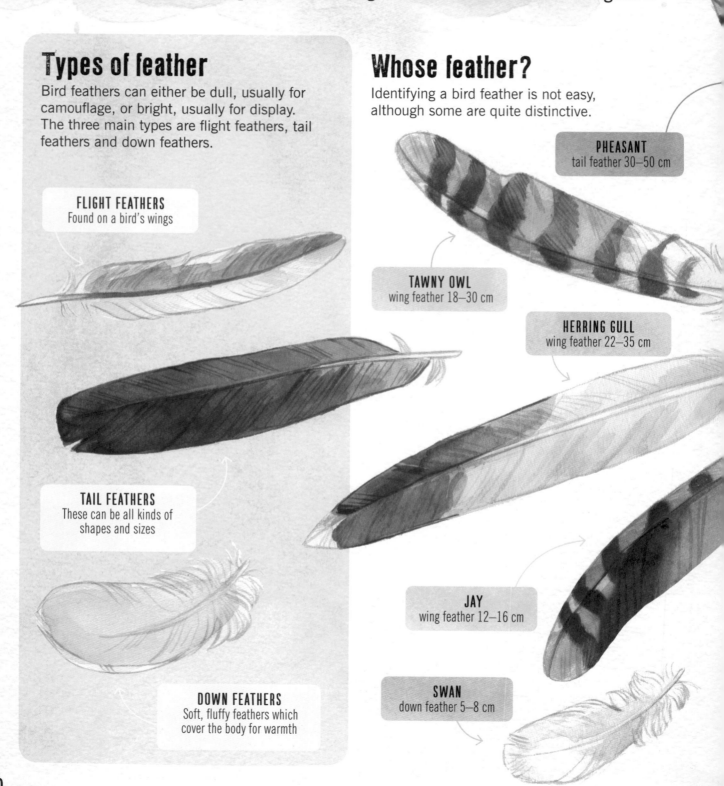

## Types of feather

Bird feathers can either be dull, usually for camouflage, or bright, usually for display. The three main types are flight feathers, tail feathers and down feathers.

**FLIGHT FEATHERS**
Found on a bird's wings

**TAIL FEATHERS**
These can be all kinds of shapes and sizes

**DOWN FEATHERS**
Soft, fluffy feathers which cover the body for warmth

## Whose feather?

Identifying a bird feather is not easy, although some are quite distinctive.

**PHEASANT**
tail feather 30—50 cm

**TAWNY OWL**
wing feather 18—30 cm

**HERRING GULL**
wing feather 22—35 cm

**JAY**
wing feather 12—16 cm

**SWAN**
down feather 5—8 cm

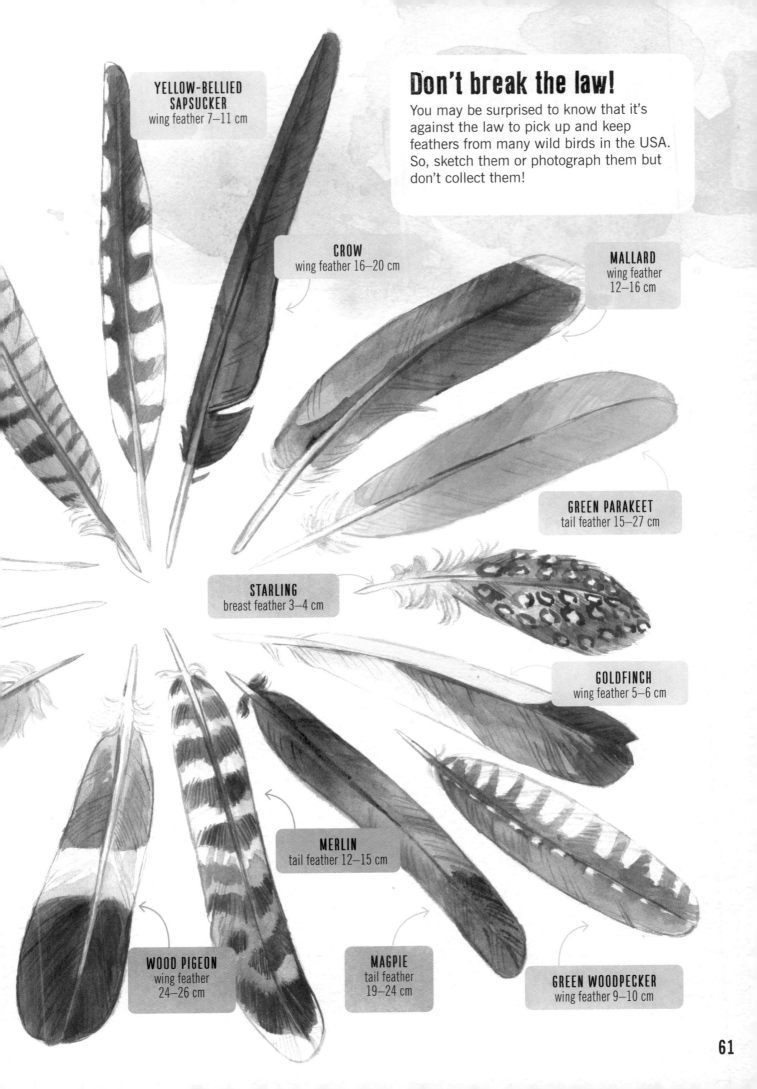

**YELLOW-BELLIED SAPSUCKER**
wing feather 7—11 cm

**CROW**
wing feather 16—20 cm

**MALLARD**
wing feather 12—16 cm

# Don't break the law!

You may be surprised to know that it's against the law to pick up and keep feathers from many wild birds in the USA. So, sketch them or photograph them but don't collect them!

**GREEN PARAKEET**
tail feather 15—27 cm

**STARLING**
breast feather 3—4 cm

**GOLDFINCH**
wing feather 5—6 cm

**MERLIN**
tail feather 12—15 cm

**WOOD PIGEON**
wing feather 24—26 cm

**MAGPIE**
tail feather 19—24 cm

**GREEN WOODPECKER**
wing feather 9—10 cm

# Whodunnit?

If you find a pile of feathers in one place it's probably the result of a predator catching and plucking a bird. There are clues to what kind of attacker might be responsible.

PEACOCK

## Leftovers

This poor bird has been captured and eaten by another animal. But what kind of creature? Read on to learn more.

## Hungry hawk

Where feathers are pulled out cleanly, this may be the work of a bird of prey, such as a sparrowhawk.

## Mammal mess

Where feathers are bitten off and bits of blood and skin are present, this is probably a killing by a mammal such as a fox. Cats also kill birds but often leave most of the body behind.

SPARROWHAWK

## Facts about feathers

- Feathers are made from the same material as our fingernails: keratin.
- Feathers have tiny hooks called barbules, enabling the flat surface to be zipped and unzipped.
- Peacocks' tail feathers are amazing colours because they reflect light in a special way.
  - Swans are believed to have the most feathers of any bird: up to 25,000!
  - Birds are often home to lice which eat their feathers. You may find that a feather you collect is eaten away over time.
  - A bird's feathers usually weigh more than its skeleton.

SWAN

# Dangerous things to track: TIGERS

Sadly, in the past so many people have tracked and hunted tigers that these majestic big cats are in danger of dying out altogether. Now tigers are tracked mainly by tourists and conservationists. Everyone has to be careful because they are FEARSOME!

## WHAT TO LOOK FOR

Tiger trackers in India look for these clues:

- ✴ Footprints
- ✴ Poo
- ✴ Scratch marks on trees
- ✴ Vultures circling a kill
- ✴ Agitated deer
- ✴ Alarm calls of monkeys

## Tiger facts

1 Tigers' main prey is deer and wild pigs but they do also eat buffalo, dogs, bears, snakes, crocodiles and leopards.

2 A tiger's roar can be heard from 3 km away.

3 There are more captive tigers in the world (pets and zoo animals) than wild tigers.

4 Unlike most cats, tigers like water and are good swimmers.

5 Tigers have striped skin as well as striped fur.

Oh deer!

## Why are they dangerous?

Tigers are among the world's largest and most powerful predators. They can kill animals twice their size and they do occasionally eat people.

# Index

# Quiz answers

Page 18:   1. c, sheep; 2. b, swan; 3. a, water vole; 4. d, elephant; 5. c, fly; 6. a, beaver.

Page 30:   1. b, weasel; 2. c, fallow deer; 3. d, crow; 4. a, leopard; 5. b, gull; 6. d, elephant.

Page 40:   1. c, badger; 2. a, harvest mouse; 3. d, beaver; 4. a, woodpecker; 5. b, wood ant; 6. d, wasp.

Page 46:   1. d, beaver; 2. a, caterpillar; 3. b, bank vole; 4. a, deer; 5. b, slug; 6. d, squirrel.